AF411969

The Double Negatives of the Living

The Double Negatives of the Living

Poems by

Gary Fincke

ℨ

ZOLAND BOOKS
Cambridge, Massachusetts

First edition published in 1992 by
Zoland Books, Inc.
384 Huron Avenue, Cambridge, MA 02138

Grateful acknowledgment is made to Oberlin College Press for permission to quote from "Brief Reflections on Floods," by Miroslav Holub, published in the Sagittal Section *of the* Field Translation Series, #3, 1980.*

Designed by Lori K Pease
Cover art by Gene Matras
Copyright ©1992 by Gene Matras

Library of Congress Catalog Card Number
91-66475
ISBN 0-944072-18-6

Library of Congress Cataloging-in-Publication Data

Fincke, Gary.
    The double negatives of the living : poetry / by Gary Fincke.
      p. cm.
    ISBN 0-944072-18-6 (pbk.) : $9.95
    I. Title.
    PS3556. I457D6 1992
    811'.54--dc20   91-66475

Acknowledgments

Some of the poems in this collection have previously appeared in the following periodicals: *Amelia, Beloit Poetry Journal, Boston Literary Review, Boulevard, The Cresset, The Gettysburg Review, Graham House Review, Green Mountains Review, The Laurel Review, Mid-American Review, The North American Review, Oxford Magazine, Painted Bride Quaterly, Poet & Critic, Poet Lore, Poetry, Poetry Northwest, Prairie Schooner, Three Rivers Poetry Journal, West Branch, Yarrow,* and *Zone 3.*

"Malthus Season" and "Tube Time" appeared in the chapbook *Handing the Sky Back*, GreenTower Press, 1990. "The Cabbage Plan" appeared in the chapbook *Breath*, State Street Press, 1984. "Put This Gown On," "Six Kinds of Music, the Wallpaper of Breasts," "Reaching the Deaf," and "The Fly" appeared in the chapbook *The Public Talk of Death*, Two Herons Press, 1991. "The AIDS List" appeared in *Poets For Life*, Crown Publishers, 1989.

Contents

"A real flood is when bubbles come from the mouth
and we think they're words."
—Miroslav Holub

The Double Negatives of the Living

Naming The Sky

"There's my sky," my father says. I don't know
What he expects, answer, in his driveway,
"It's clear, all right," and idling in neutral,
Think he's planning to tell me the ancient
Names for the dots or the tales they fathered,
People who suffered, changed, and ascended
While somebody handed their stories down.
Two dippers and Orion—I forget
The rest or never learned or failed to see
Anything but the stars scattered on our scale
Of pulse and breath. I want him to show me
Archer, bear, lion; I want marble busts
Of myth to form above us like pillars
Of flame, chariots of fire, accounting
For every light, and because my mother
Has died, wonder if he means to show me
Where she is, how one cluster has reformed
To suggest a melodrama of hope.
Heavy-headed with travel, I wait while
The time-released light, set to eleven,
Blinks off in his living room like stars near
The horizon tumbling off the sky's screen.
And I remember no clock in this house
Is correct, all six set so fast no one
Would believe them, early as wet robins
In today's false thaw of February.
We stand with the night in our lungs; we breathe

A sentence of silence until he says,
"Venus and Jupiter," directs me low
In the sky where I see so many lights
I can nod, certain they are among them.

The Flower Remedies

1

"Are flowers thinking?" my son asked once.
"Do they know who we are?" and I worried
For his manhood, wished he'd requested
A translation for snarls, the idioms
Of growls. "They know us like the newly born,"
I told him. "If they breathed, they would cry."

2

Nothing could keep Edward Bach from flowers.
Not scoffing. Not weather. Not the symptoms
He showed when he approached the proper plants:
Hatred near holly; beside mustard, gloom.
So sensitive, Bach was, he imagined
Self-pity by chicory; guilt at pine.
They healed him, healed the distress of others
Who drank his flower teas. Take cerato
For self-doubt; taste iris for frustration;
Then smile, sip aspen for anxiety,
Whisper, "Bach," say, "The Flower Remedies."

3

I hear my wife say her student, today,
Sat up barking, and she thought, like her class,
He was joking, a first-day-of-school test
For his teacher. "He was growling," she says.
"He sounded so much a dog I thought it

Was talent." Under the table our Spitz
Lies listening to what it knows; already
I want to say "Well?" but my wife offers
The syndrome's name for bad luck in the genes:
Snarl, spit, what the old exorcists knew.
Our dog waits to sit and beg, but no one
Is holding food. The house trick it's mastered—
Not to be deceived by one thing at least,
Thinking in barks and growls like a student.

4
To believe in the brain's
many routes from disease;
to learn stress buffers;
to read this week's book
on meditation, stretching,
deep breathing and joy.
"Rock rose for panic, gorse
for despair"—each day is
pocked with moods; what we
become has walked in others
and still we study. Choler,
we read—bile, phlegm, blood—
so medieval in another
smug week of solutions.

5
I am walking to work, thinking of flowers. How few I recognize.
The roadside is littered with mysteries, and I know as little about
the cars that brush my walking. I need a lesson in America, in

goods, in the names for constructed things, and I say, "Cerato, iris, aspen" to begin the multiplication of forgetfulness. I would turn into these fields if I remembered the identity clues—color, shape, pattern, number—everything leaves and petals, each of my terrors swept away by the undertow of flowers.

Opening The Locks

*In 1968, Dr. Ian Stevenson suggested that the old and the dying
send him combination locks to be opened after their deaths through
friends communicating with their spirits.*

Immediately, Dr. Stevenson had takers,
New locks carefully boxed, laid in cotton
And tissue beside the names of the living
Who'd be willing to listen for spirits
They'd known to send the combinations.
And last week my father opened a safe
In his garage, repeating left 40, right 30,
Left 20, right 10, twice to zero and open,
A simple countdown to bonds and deeds
And a collection of coins. He had me
Write it down; he wasn't joking about
The lapse he thought I'd have, and neither
Was Stevenson when he directed the aging
To memorize their six numbers, giving them
Mnemonics for the dead: IN EDEN HEAVEN
NO HELL LIVING ANGELS. "There's no sense
Forgetting," he said, "no point in shouting
The wrong digits across space and time."
And some of us, at least, are teaching
Ourselves memory tricks, resurrection
Sentences like WE GO ON and WE LIVE
To make sure the locks we leave are opened.
One hundred twenty-five thousand to one
Are the odds, I've been told, in the paradise
Lottery. This week the odds are worse

To win twelve million dollars in Pennsylvania's
Jackpot, yet the lines to buy tickets
Curve through the mall, nothing, I think,
Like waiting to touch the mourning locks,
Attentive to the dead and the signals
They might be sending. And lately,
Some of the survivors have gathered
To listen, hearing *four* or *forty*
Or far away traffic, twirling their dials
And tugging each Sargent and Greenleaf
Like a knot, like a sword in stone,
Cursing like the unchosen when they lose
The pick six of the afterlife. And there
Are times when all of us hear combinations
As we dress or dream, when the numbers
Seem to be chanted along waves of light,
The sequence simple as the mathematics
Of the nursery, the addition and subtraction
Of eat and sleep. Listen, listen, listen,
We tell ourselves, and expect, suddenly,
To hear tumblers, have something solved
In our lives. And then, driven, press
Our ears to the future, listening again
To hear a second voice, verification,
The start of all locks sliding free
As if each one is touched by eternity.

The Conversation Of Elephants

Someone's listened like a spy, worn a wire
Among the giants and labeled thirty
Elephant calls, deciphering bellow,
Trumpet, and roar. "We've just scratched the surface,"
Elephant experts say, and I'd agree,
Listening to my groans and snorts and screams
To hear some small fraction of what I mean.

And when elephants talk, we've learned, they send
Part of their speech in secret. They rumble
Reminders along an inaudible
Frequency while we write the elephant
Myths of memory, attribute the great,
Swaying regrouping of herds to something
Besides the hummed prompt to muscle and bone.

And those elephants, we've confirmed, discuss
Contempt for humans. Those bulls and cows thrum,
"Avoid or trample," splitting strategies,
Discouraging the eavesdroppers along
The strange, infrasound frequencies of God,
Who keeps us from overhearing his voice
Through the buzz and vibration of each day,

The sound-shifting we manage, like the death
Of silent letters, the lost consonants
Of *gnaw* and *hymn*, *psalm* and *phlegm*, threatened by

Demand's simple spellings, those marvels turned
Phonetic as the sweet, syrupy sobs
For trivial loss that replace the cries
Which have calcified, unused, in our hearts.

The Stuttering Cures

One thing we learn: how much poison
The body can take. Alcohol,
For instance. Cruelty. Prayer as duty.
Once a day Ronnie Muller read
History aloud because Mrs. Cook
Demanded a paragraph
Of recitation. Stuttering's cure,
Perhaps, though Ronnie Muller,
Force-fed like a protest faster,
Never finished a sentence
Before P or T swallowed
His breath and the carburetor
In his throat stalled for good.

And always, there's worse, some surgeon
A hundred years before Mrs. Cook who
Snipped portions of stutterers' tongues,
Clipped strategic bits and pieces
Like speech therapy's barber.

All of those stories of stutterers
Who can sing, who can whisper,
Who can perfectly speak in unison
Or when they cannot hear themselves:
Each one of those patients, after
The plastic surgery for speech,
Waited for that doctor to unwrap

His transformed tongue, to say, "Yes, now,"
As welcome. Think of that first
Tentative stutter, the patient
Hearing imperfection's nuance,
The misery of misdirected breath
Lengthening to the wish for
The speechless life of stone.

So easily, the wind we've stored
Scatters the memos of our thinking.
The man who sold me insurance
Lost his tongue to cancer, entered
The enormous stammer of silence,
The messages on his note pad
Thinning to *yes* and *no*, to tapping,
At last, on the empty tablet,
Nothing anyone could decipher,
As if it were a personal code
Or all of his thoughts now stuttered.

Scorecards

This is the summer the nine-hundred line
To Elvis is open. For two dollars
You can listen to him say, "I'm not dead,"
That soon he'll be singing to the faithful
Just like Jesus, though the hotline to him
Starts higher than a couple of dollars,
What I'm reading right now in a letter
From the parish. It says I owe God more;
It says I need to double what I give
Because their computer tells them my job
Is worth it, assessing like an audit
Or the sad chorus of a country song.

I stick it on the refrigerator,
Tape it beside my son's SAT scores
And the cholesterol counts in red meat.
And so far, three hundred thousand people
Have called Elvis. And lately I've spent hours
Wired straight to my familiar, recent dead,
And none of their voices have hummed rebirth
While the greenhouse effect keeps me inside,
Turns joggers to walkers, turns my neighbors
Into sentries for water, so silent
And distant they might be burglars equipped
With a wonderful disguise. And among
Such strangers who might run their fingers down
Their scorecards to find my name and my size,

My age, my wife, and where I'm positioned;
I'm talking to them in the voice we hear
When we imagine ourselves as others.

Parables

At the end of our lot ten seedlings, six
Cabbage, and the stump starts of raspberry,
This year's sprout farm where I've dug and planted
Whatever I've been given by neighbors.
All summer, mowing, I'll pass them, and some
Will shoot green, some wither, and some, stillborn,
Never change at all. I know so little
About gardening I cannot place blame.
Near the maple I mow a hundred sprouts
Each week; the crown vetch from the county land
Leaps and clutches as if the untended
Could rear like doom or like parables, like
Tough Eddie Downing and Mickey Conti
And every held-back hoodlum in ninth grade.
They had sideburns; they wore leather; they put
Their hands on the breasts of the girls who leaned
Against them in the halls, and the summer
After they quit school, I lifted a pick
And the heavy stone-age head of it slammed
The smooth-shaft length to my astonished hand.
"Dammit, Christ, shit!" I shouted, and was slapped
By the small size of my cut, the silence
Of my father that lasted the three days
We worked to mold the straight trench for sidewalks.
I was nowhere close to disabled, to
Cigarettes and beer and opened thighs, but
Suddenly I wanted to be shallow
Enough to lay myself down like cement,

Harden and flourish as quickly as Christ's
Examples before some quirk of blights scythed
My thin body. And sometimes now I sit
On my curb and feel the brown-bagged bottle
Settle in my dry hand, see the tight skirts
Of my neighborhood rising while I turn
Into fable, green gone to brown, thinking
Of the million seeds beneath this asphalt,
The machinery those roadworkers used,
The kind of wounds they took from their mistakes,
The obscenities those wounds demanded.

Walking

For Miles
These are the nights
when it takes four miles
to slow because the cat
or your children stuff
each room with sound
that catches dark under
your nails; because
your mother has called,
cross country, to tell
you how fluid settles
in her as if the shallow
breaths she is taking
condense and sink
to her ankles to keep
her from walking;
and there's nothing
you can do to keep
from retracing your hike
but turn into
some farmer's field,
sort out one row
between these stalks
and rattle forward
because nobody plants,
you think, these things
in a circle.

The Dog

This time you're walking
north on a block
of boarded windows.
Left to the river;
right to the railroad.
At the corner a man
dressed as a child
rocks on a bicycle.
"Uh-huh, uh-huh," he says,
answering the queries
of the missing. The dog
you're walking lifts
its ears. One-handed,
you think which store
might be open. At the end
of the list it's evening
in a town of old children.

In Cadence

Like this band. Like files
and columns driven by drums
of an old-fashioned army.
Like the last believers
who obeyed "Keep rank" and
the whistle for the sprint
through no-man's land.
And your room, as you listen
to this beat, goes black

with the cumulus gathering
of uniforms. Here you are
rising to the window
for the lurch of parade.
Here you are sick and steadying
yourself like a tourist,
like Zapruder braced to film
his small share of a motorcade.

To Work

In the field you cross, stockings
that you test with your shoe.
And they're knotted. And you think
strangler, rapist, the man who might
long to wear them. And in all this
mown grass, even in the darkness
gone west, nowhere to hide the acts
you imagine. And you bend to retrieve
them, to carry with you this evidence
of what happens when you're not walking
to work, your car in the driveway like
your dog in the large window staring
your figure into the landscape where
it meets the buildings you work inside
with stockings balled in your pocket.

Into Thin Air

Where Enoch walked. Where, you've read,
David Long the farmer went, his friends

waving as he vanished from his field.
"Sure, we're sure," they testified,
although they no longer knew the meaning
of David Long; although, surrounded
on all sides by logic, they repeated
the evidence of his circle: lush grass,
no insects, no animal who would enter
that pale plane of ascension but men
who chanced anything, listening for
the voice of the lost. Although the friends,
when they dreamed of David Long, saw him
mute and waving, saw him vanish soundless.

At The Reception In Our Yard

I am listening to our guest
say, *"el oscuro,"* and he adds,
because we ask, that some men
spend a year squatting
in the darkness solitary
that sits four by four
like a crawl-in closet,
more than enough, I think,
to atrophy muscles into
a permanent beggar's crouch;
and much of our crowd files
this kind of violence under
"distant" or "unthinkable"
like a colonel's bag of ears
or the carnage in the film
my sons have rented because
it holds a world's record,
one hundred and thirty-four
acts of violence per hour,
invasion by killers who shoot
when anyone approaches
saying, "What's the problem?"
And when it begins to rain
we crouch and cover and rush
inside to stand together
behind a wall's length
double pane of glass I own

to use better the sun
when it hangs south of here,
throwing noon light on talk
like ours turned bone,
some of us watching
our share of slaughter
over the shoulders of my sons,
and I want one of us
to say, "kill or be killed,"
casual as "go fuck yourself"
or "we get what we deserve,"
and then up to our eyeballs
we'd be in the literal
hammer and nails, hinge and lock,
mood, weather, the wish
of our worst arming itself,
shallow and labored as
a critical psalm of breathing.

Reaching The Deaf

Screams of distress are in the vocal spectrum
least affected by age deterioration. (Extraordinary Endings)

I've cursed behind my mother,
Spent my rage-list of phrases
While she scrubbed grease from plates.
My father, now, hears nothing
On his right, and I've tested him
With blasphemy from the shotgun seat.
And I've settled, full front,
For vague heresies, measured
My lies by volume, but here is
The news of Gertrude Jameison,
Eighty-five, harrassing
Doug Thompson forty-six years,
Calling him eight times a day
Despite court orders, four months
At a penal farm, and a lock
On her phone. Nothing's stopped her.
Not a stroke. Not confinement
In a nursing home. Not Thompson
Gone so silent on the line
She asks if he knows her, if he
Has something to say, shrill
With still guessing the phrase
To stop his heart. Some screams
Must run the painted needle to
The North of the penny compass.

Some distress must sing itself
Up the noon or midnight
Of the gumball clock. Think of
The way a woman calls and calls;
How another waters her lawn
All day for a year, swamping
Herself and her neighbors, what
She means to say in her faucet,
The sum of her language forming
A shrieking wetlands. Think how
The pulse of imminence searches
Through things in common, speeding us to
The bestial vowels that reach the deaf.

The Phone Call

A woman driving through Harrisburg
sees her husband by the highway. She calls

my house because I live closest, and he
is dead. "He's in Enola," she tells me,

and I know she hears my music. The light
is bad in December; I squint across

the road where she should pass, New York
on her mind. "He's still the same," she says,

and I think how fourteen years is enough,
of the characteristics of change,

that Enola, stretched along the railroad,
is no place where anyone would sleep.

I tell her to visit. I check the clock
while she refuses. "He was unmarked,"

she says, and then, "thank you," rushing away
from my answer that spirals slowly through

the cord. Like his plane would look from the ground,
time enough to pull out of any explosive tumble.

The Fly

I tell my son, driving him to school,
That the wind this morning is like Buffalo's.
He looks for his friends, has nothing to say
About where he's never lived, though last night
He babbled through dinner about the fly
In our kitchen, how he felt sorry
For something so doomed by timing.
He wanted me to let it live,
So sluggish I caught it with a jar.
"It's a mistake," I said, but he held
That jar while we talked about the boy
In his class who'd been electrocuted
In his bathtub, a lamp tumbling
In with him while his parents watched t-v.
"There were lights in the bathroom," the mother
Said in the paper, "so maybe it was for heat."
And my son must have been thinking
About how cold his baths have been,
How he's popped out of the water and wrapped
Himself in his thick, cartoon towels.
Before he runs to the playground,
I want to tell him about walking backwards
Into the '77 blizzard that put Buffalo
On television for a week, how I made
A mile in it, foolish with weather
While my body whispered to me
Every frozen man's story of sleep.

How I finished my drowsy countdown
Through those ten blocks, shoving my heels
Toward home. And instead I say something
About flys, how sometimes they buzz
Back to life underneath a sun-shot window,
Which was where we'd dumped his, postponing
At least one choice this winter insists on.

The Pet Cemetery

It was the kind of place
I walked with a notebook,
A grant supporting me
Cross country. I copied
Down inscriptions that were
Parodies and wondered
What anyone driving
Route 80 would think of
Edgar Friedell paying
Somebody to inscribe
BAMBI WAS MY BABY
On a headstone. I thought
Of how I was spending
Pennsylvania's money,
Believing I could find
Poems daily by starting
My car, and remembered
The fat anthologies
I carried, the number
Of fellowship winners
Like myself who filled up
American highways
Until they found one place
That convinced them they were
Alone. I walked down past
OUR LOST LITTLE GIRLIE
And MY SWEETIE and stood

On the shoulder the way
I did before I thought
About poems or how much
One of those drivers could
Make me pay for a ride,
And I kept guessing how
I looked to every man
Or woman who might be
Watching for hitch-hikers,
And Christ, I wanted to
Heave that notebook across
The highway, one more tax
Dollar symbol, and I
Wanted Edgar Friedell
To show up with flowers
So I could ask him how
He'd done it, loved something
Enough to sign his name.

The Flat Earth

"New Haven city officials acknowledge there was a gap between the two-ton concrete barriers on a closed road where a car plunged into a river, killing all four occupants, but they don't know if anyone is to blame." (AP)

1

"Who moved the barriers?"
the spokesman said. "When?"

2

We drove, with our murmurs, to work.
We parked and locked, and our colleague,
We learned, had been killed by a skid
Through her windshield. It may have fallen
From a truck; it may have been struck
And sent airborne. We looked up *skid*
In the dictionary and stared at the killer
On the lineup of its page. The names
For things, the identities we give them
As if there were a literature of wood.
After the chaos of wrong turns, what
Is there to do during the silence
Where our schooling lives? How do we read
While the hearsay of the morning darkens?

3

In the first days of our house, into
Its empty lot, we planted trees so

Something would say we're home. We waited
For leaves until every nearby tree
Was green, until we'd handicapped
The chances of ours catching in June,
None of us placing a bet that our
Branches would answer the color wish.

The birds that settled for seeds pecked
Clear of those bone shadows, and in
The evenings of summer the world famine
Broke out in our part of Pennsylvania
Like measles, lay in pin-points
On our personal landscape as if,
Uprooting, we'd traced the logic
Of a serial killer: The lost oak,
The beech, the maple. There were more holes
In our yard we could dig; the earth
In each place was as safe as someone
Beginning any uneventful day.

4

This morning I walked the dotted-line accident route from the
newspaper photo. To street's end. To where a bridge belongs or
the planet should curve and continue so drivers don't plunge
toward dragons. Nearby, a man scanned the ground for scrap,
for change; and I would have believed him, in that moment, if he
had insisted he was sweeping for buried mines beside that river
where a bridge runs parallel to its banks, points downstream/
upstream like the flat persona for a detour that sends drivers to
drowning.

5

This article says
the earth is flat,
the earth is plane,
doesn't spin like
the child's ball in
the science myths.
In the fables
of astronomers
we are whirling.
On the cracker
of fact, we're gods
who quest for limits,
and, finding none,
know the saltine
we've inherited
can walk our folklore
feet toward faith.

6

In New Haven, the map has a lie
Of red, a field of possible coins,
But finally I had to drive west,
Sprint home avoiding the oceans
At the brink of our highways.
I drowsed past my exit; I took
A strange two lanes, apprehensive
At once as if they were testament
That might suddenly lurch to the side,

Unwilling to go forward where
The world might end. What destroys us—
A flung raft of planks, an abutment
Moved like pillars in Gaza . . .

At the first shadowed curve I braked
Hard and panic-heavy and thought
This is how we shatter, how we
Tumble into the astonishment
Of falling as if the wafer
Of our world has cracked like promise.
On one side of the earth there is silence;
On one side of the earth we are weightless.
As I stopped, my body sped into
The seat belt; at the ragged edge
Of the earth, the snap of its holster
Sung in the dark like the living.

Malthus Season

This week, or last, or seven months ago,
The world's five billionth person was born,
And my children, this morning, sail with me
To Heart Island where eight million names
Are scribbled on Boldt Castle's wreck of walls
As if *The Naked City* had signed in,
Please, to tell its secrets for money.
For now, we're guest panelists touring
One of the Thousand Islands, its ruin
So much a cemetery I work the dates
Backward to "Albert Chester, 1912,"
So early a vandal he might have had
Windows to break, paneling to peel,
Time to search seventy-seven rooms
To validate his signature as first.
And nearby is "Take Notice, 1932,"
Inside a balloon speaking for the Crofts:
Herman, Lorraine, Caroline and Calvin.
And maybe they were the millionth name,
Something like the world this week, t-shirts
On sale, the population tallied
Like hamburgers or the world's record
Of Mary Faulkner, the woman who wrote
Nine hundred and four novels, setting
A standard for typing. She used six
Different names; I could write any name
In this room but mine, claiming to love Sue

And Carrie and Shannon until my arm
Tired from working the guest book of these walls
Where surely there is someone I know,
The time correct like "Sharon Loves Gary,
1961," coincidence of desire
For one year I cared about Sharon too shy
To scrawl unless, I begin to think,
Foolish as Boldt building this relic,
1904, she had such a passion,
Her signature, that summer, rustling
Inside her purse until it lurched to
Eye level like "Puerto Rican Spirit,
The Bronx, 1957," sprayed so large
It might be true, making myths from these walls,
Turning ourselves heroes or at least
Decipherable names like Heart Island,
Reconstructed so even the literal
Can see this valentine from the air.

The Train Cure

In some parts of Egypt, people believe lying face down on a railroad
track and letting a train pass over you will cause an abortion.

The trains come infrequently, or not at all,
And she has brought nothing to eat or drink.
Certainly, there are no schedules posted,
No switchmen for this track that opens a sigh
Through the country, each hour postponed
Until there is none but the one where she
Holds a calendar, examines her watch, keeps
A running total of her countdown. Waiting,
She thinks the child moves in her future,
Crawls, and then, horribly, walks. Only
The track's whisper, she says, the approach
Of instruments. In this story of solutions,
Where vibration means something must happen,
She chooses her place carefully, slams shut
Her eyes, and grips the ground to keep her head
Heavy with trust, thick with thrust enough
To deliver a grave in the discipled earth.

In Emerico's Bar

In Emerico's Bar a man
becomes my classmate again,
drinking his way to the desk
across from me in physics.
"A bunch of ball bearings
on strings," he recalls,
"and ripples to measure
in water," while I watch
the Pirates collapsing
on the forty-four inch screen
and a woman who might have sat,
ten years later, between the same
tuning forks that we had, learning
about the silent spots in sound.

"None of it's coming back,"
he says, switching to steel,
and I nod as he shows me
his hands are less calloused
than mine that cut grass,
hold a racket on weekends
two hundred miles east
of the next Pirate error,
an overthrow that scores
a runner from first.
Trajectory, I think,
speed and angle and the uniform

curve that balls must travel,
and he starts listing
the dead names of our class.

Accidents and Vietnam.
Enough for this roster,
but he keeps it up:
"The heart and cancer,
that's what's after us now,"
and I can't disagree,
remembering the momentum
of those marbles, how their arcs
narrowed while we calculated
whatever had been assigned.
Like polarity, I think,
watching the woman lean
away from the bar, swaying
a little as if the doorway
behind her led to song.

Tube Time

Late in the National Anthem hours,
The channels switching suddenly to snow,
You could stay awake, in 1960,
For the last B-movie of the early
Morning, a formula it took minutes
To confirm, and then, before the climax,
A final ad for discount furniture
Or a furnace. "Three rooms, three ninety-eight,"
Sang a woman who was supposed to be
Newlywed, crooning into her blessed house
From a porch swing as if she'd discovered
The aphrodisiac for progress.
And next up, Pie Traynor, the white-haired
Hall of Fame third baseman forlornly
Reading his lines beside the boxed way
To heat cheaply those marked-down furnished rooms.
"Who can?" a voice intoned from nowhere,
And Pie, from the Hot Corner, answered,
"Ameri-can." Nothing varied during
Tube time but the sequels to Bulova,
1941, the first t-v ad
In the sell series that showed you how to
Measure the shards of your life. "What will
They do when they run out of ideas?"
My mother asked, and I said, "They won't"
Like a son, but I'm counting on them, now,
To be eternal, a non-stop story

Stitched along seams of sales. I know
I've been afraid of television snow,
That I've flicked through the disconnected
Cable cycle of them sweating that next
Was news of the atomic war. I've thought
Time after time that Conelrad would
Replace the lost comedies, and I think
It now, renewing relief in the patch
Of canned figures busy with dialogue
That says nothing about the vaporized
End of man. And then the need to question
A second channel to make sure this film
Isn't the last ignorant sit-com
In America, somehow beaming
A lie like three furnished rooms you'll loathe,
Like Pie Traynor stiff from shilling,
Like a photographic negative
For a gun game: one empty chamber,
Five live rounds, putting it to your head
And thinking, in the snow of pause, how this
Is what it means to be a believer.

Breaking Glass

Each Saturday I hurled
Ant-crusted pop bottles
Into Pine Creek, betting
Whether they would shatter,
Catching a stone in the shallows.

And right there, from the bank,
A huge mouth of pipe coughed
Sewage into the creek,
The foam breaking up and
Floating toward the Allegheny.

"The mill's shit," Aunt Margaret
Would say, and let me test
Another bottle while
She balanced A&P
Bags on the Butler Street railing.

Which was the road we walked,
Where the planned bypass would
Bottleneck, the drivers
Cursing lines stalled over
Sharpsburg on a thin, suspect bridge.

Somebody was found in
The water one Sunday,
Somebody whom no one

Identified, and just
Beside the place in the photo,

The water frothing through
The rocks, I hung onto
The sumac and looked back
Into the drooling pipe,
Defying the mill's fat body.

From inside, a thick wind;
From above, the sumac
Shoving me like someone
Just freed from a shattered
Bottle. When I crawled up the bank,

The dark, blood-heavy humus slid
Back behind me into the creek.

Night Work

What my father said to me, keeping
The worst of himself silent
In the white-breath bakery evenings,
Was nothing that stayed, caught up
On my shoulders like a hunchback's curse.
Which was his gift, those phrases
That flickered like moths and flew
Into the morning sun, leaving me
Shift-end light, though once,
Behind the bakery, in mid-winter,
The light powder snow so cold
And unsettled, a drunk fell in the alley
And believed quicksand had him to the hips.
"Baker!" he cried, recognizing
The swamp smell of dough.
"Baker, baker!" a chant in the sinking night,
And my father counted his need
Like a pulse until the thready thump
Of his name drummed him outside.

In the chair by the display case
The drunk sugar-dreamed his way
Toward morning, and when, carrying rolls,
My father returned, he had melted
Into the floor, lost in one
Of those spontaneous holes
That open in the irrational Earth.

And even now, I can tell, side-stepping,
How agility is important, how
The long night snow covers the holes
Underfoot. "Baker," I sometimes mumble,
And test my footing, not ready to trust
Whoever might be awake, his hands busy
Inside the rising, dependent dough.

The Cabbage Plan

The snow, the cabbage
Lost in December
Like skulls under
Our sleds, and the question
I wanted to ask
Was why the cabbage
Had been left behind
As if the farmer
Wanted his losses
Counted or he planted
Something inedible
Each sacrificial year.
I have meant,
Occasionally, to read
About rotation
Or parasites
Or the farmer
Become famous, growing
An original crop
Between the rank heads
Because my children
Hate cabbage, because
They applaud his choice,
And taste seals itself
In ice and believes
In its field-hard walls.

Open Field Tackle

First he took the snap
from himself and pivoted,
handing off and churning
the tucked ball upfield
through the trap-blocked hole.
It was an offense, that fall,
built on the run, the tailback
over four yards a carry,
the sticks made, short yardage,
by throwing himself under
the hedges where the lawn stopped.

But some plays he spun
and feinted so smoothly
he knew he'd broken free,
skittering the trip back
across the yard, reversing,
reversing again, thirty,
forty, fifty, hearing
the radio's hoarse crescendo
say forty, thirty, and catch
on twenty-five, his last
nearly full-circle spin
flinging him forward
and down, the ball protected
from the open-field tackle
so incredible through
his knees and ankles.

All October he played
every offensive snap,
going both ways and never
breaking one clean.
His statistic rules kept
it one chance per season,
maybe, the way it was,
nothing over eighty yards,
not even when his team
was down six, a minute
to go, unless someone
missed an assignment,
sprang him free on the fly,
the ball spiraling up
in front of him, lying
on the ends of his fingers
so much like the perfect pass
he kept those reversals going:
forty, thirty, twenty, ten,
and then the outflung hand
just catching his heel,
the three-sixty in the air,
the reaching out with the ball,
so close to the goal line
he had to turn his head,
mid-air, to read the eyes
that were checking for breaks
in that imaginary plane.

The End Of Ganster Street

The stories that stay are about scars
In places where no one traces
Their length, leaving the shirt
Tucked in over a scene like the end
Of Ganster Street buried by the bypass,
A gorge opening that motorist summer
When we watched truckloads of chickens
Empty into the last Croatian butcher shop,
The one where the cats lurked, the one
Where the thick men danced a hog shuffle
Through blood that could have poured
From the dying street. All of us
Waited for the rock slide and missed it
As we slept. Later, standing apart
From our parents, we watched
The mud-flecked men search for bodies,
Turning, like our town, into
Women at the mouth of a mine.

Shoveling The Beans

I applied for work, walked
Into a boxcar to pitch beans
Torn loose from bags. A shift
Of coughing. A primer for asthma
Or emphysema, the future named
By consequence, but I made
Money because no long-timer
Would carry the shovel inside.

Nobody worked my break. I hung
Out a window and chased breath
By myself, figuring, sometimes,
How long I'd last if I lived
On that riverfront street where
Everybody, waiting for the sun
To fall, bunched up in doorways.

Ahead of me was college and
Three months more of bags broken
By travel toward the warehouse
Where sucking grime was expected,
But I never saw an engine, and
Those cars, after a while, could
Have been dropped from the sky,
My brain clouded by bean-dust
Until I could be as deceived
As the first film audience who

Thought their locomotive was
Rumbling out of the wall at them.

The engine's steam spilled up
In clouds. One by one those people
Saw their fundamental fears
Turn dwarfish. And all summer
Things shrank until only
My calendar was in that fog.
Beside the time clock, the last day,
I watched expressions to find
The stunned look settling on
Whoever would shovel next,
Someone who'd shovel for years,
Who'd recognize the beans
By shape and color, repeating
Pinto, navy, kidney, pink,
Knowing each of them by dust,
Their fingerprints swirling
Around him like a million clues
For a cheap and simple crime.

The Nazi On The Phone

No one expects to die
for his language, falling
into the news because
of a gesture or symbol,
but in 1970 you could dial
propaganda, a quarter
for three minutes about
Commies and Catholics,
Niggers and Kikes. "We have
a mandate," the blond voice said,
"to never betray ourselves,"
and you could find, if you asked,
the false storefront in Akron.
That May someone I knew
had been dropped by a volley
from the National Guard.
I was starting a thesis;
I was using the Kent State
campus to put more distance
between me and every factory
I passed while I grew.
It was 1970, and my uncles
wished for their World War
rifles because the protests
went on. My hair was a flag,
and in the mornings I ran
three miles and reconsidered

Nietzche and Schopenhauer.
No one ran but me, though once
when the early bus rolled by
I remembered cross-Pittsburgh
road trips, how each one of us
on our all-white track team
screamed "coon" and "spade"
up the alleys where we would
never live, and during
the last quarter mile I guessed
their unheard answers, ducking
and pushing myself from
the past's thin windows when
I was sure of their reply.

During the First Semester

One student wrote about ambush,
How slaughter found the four men
Closest to him below Tayninh.
I gave him a B—faulty tense,
Comma splices—something that showed
I knew what I was hired for.

He revised the next one,
"The Virtues of Karate,"
Because his father was a master,
Because he was practicing,
And before more essays were due
He dueled his father and strangled
Him with nunchaku.
                              The report
Said they fought forty-five minutes,
A long time to kill someone
Hand to hand. I'd call it a draw;
I'd say enough and walk away
Though I've never trained to see
How lethal I might be
If I had spurs, if I heard
The goad of being surrounded.

Maybe both of them flashed back
To their wars, going mad in Asia.
Maybe the son had to prove

He was not the only loser
In America. He may have tried
To breathe the air in that room
Back into his father, may have
Pinched the nape of his neck,
Blown into his throat as if
It were a downed rooster's vent,
Something else I've read about,
Thinking about nunchaku,
How farm tools are fashioned
Into weapons, how hands and feet,
Finally, are not enough.

Scratch Test

The allergist says,
"This will be cold,
then colder, and smell,"
what acetone does,
I suppose, lying
on my stomach with
a *Reader's Digest*.
Thirty-seven pricks
in the back. I count them
the way I sum up
everything. Numbers help.
The issue I'm holding
is three years old.
I was breathing then.
I was running four miles
a day and counting
the seconds instead of
listening to everything
behind my rib cage.

Here is an article,
the doctor gone, about
one more maddening illness.
The woman trips. She faints
and falls and slurs
her explanation until
she barks. There's more.

Her courage, a comeback
through electric signals,
but this horror could live
anywhere along the nerves,
miles of looking for
the weak connection.

I find out I'm lucky
with this itching
I cannot reach. It says
cats and hamsters and dust,
what my house is full of,
so I will empty my life,
room by room, until
free breathing returns,
until I hear something
besides myself and
believe its importance.

The AIDS List

At breakfast, the AIDS list,
A magazine cover of faces;
On the front porch a possum
Half-grown and dead and my cat
Looking from kill to me before
Dodging *The People's Almanac*,
Heavy enough to make me killer,
Too, triple cruelty this morning,
Drawn to my doorway by the screams
Of schoolchildren. And I think
Chipmunk, rabbit, mouse, bird—
The slaughter list, something like
The lists on the flapped-open page:
20 Illegitimate Children;
12 People Who Disappeared
And Were Never Found. Although
Patty Hearst returned, I know,
And so will my cat with another kill,
Feathers or fur, gifts from the genes
Like DaVinci, Dumas, Strindberg, Wagner,
Four of the twenty love children,
The cat squalling its list
Of complaints from the shrubbery
As if research were as simple
As lust, as if it were insurance
For what we think we need to know.

The Afternoon Of Separation

All I see is this lawn turning to insects,
The brown grass becoming six-legged,
The broad-leafed weeds going hard-backed as beetles.
There are bare spots to follow, footprints
From the dance studio, and there is music
That drives me to them, that groans loudly
In the heat-wave while I go forward, sideways,
Forward, back; the insects reverting
To grass, reverting to the voiced trill of wings
Thrumming unseen among the plaintain
And the dandelion, and I am taking
The packed earth trail into the field of sumac
And milkweed where the thistle turns fierce
With scavenger's teeth, where the thick burdock stares
At roadside kills. I study a year's
Wild growth as I pass, naming the ground cover
That wants my ankles, that settles for
Every inch to the highway and my walking
Alone to the tree start of darkness
Where I can measure the brown strength of branches,
The predator in each muscled trunk,
The distances between us, the length this day
Requires to hike me to the tree line
Where every frosted thing returns to the past,
Shelled and creeping, one-celled and feeding,
Finally, on nothing but the iced weather
Of the glacier to which I'm pointed.

Put This Gown On

The long march of the parking lot,
The Epiphany rain so odd,
And thinking, thinking the thin route
To the hospital should have small
Whirlpools of flurries, the patch ice
That demands the eyes downward.

So cold, a state's width from here,
But the blizzard of this morning
Slings sideways through the changing room,
And I find a belt hooked through
Its buckle, hung and forgotten
By someone slowing his CAT-scan,
By someone sliding it pointless
Through six loops of his trousers.

And I think, undoing my pants,
His widow must watch the weather,
The first to see where the highway
Freezes, the bridge that will fishtail
The careless or doughnut the man
Who drives to deliver a belt,
The one she can't see no matter
How many mornings she's opened
His closet, closed it, and not found
Why its order is unsound.

The Slow Learners Get Shoes For School

Three sisters, they've come with their mother
To get ready for school, and my son fits them.
He brushes their ankles and speaks of leather
Lasting, the waterproof strength of stitching.
The mother listens like someone who's learned
To hear the sense in babble. She's watching
Her daughters and counting up their comfort
When they stand, when they stumble unbalanced
By this change in size, all suddenly laughing
At the silly steps around them while my son
Says, "How do they feel?" "There's the mirror,"
And they begin a dance, shuffle and skip like
They're breaking them in, like they've been bought
And carried home in boxes that surprise them
Again in the kitchen where their mother will
Watch them cakewalk their share of the source
Of dance that lurches and glides, pivots and slides.
My son is speaking to the mother; he's offering,
"Cinderella" and "Dorothy," and she answers,
"The three little kittens have found their mittens,"
And he tries to remember their names and fails,
And thinks, in his storybook, they had no tails.

Tumblebug

Stuck watching the Tumblebug arch and spin
Its way through the ride before yours, you
Memorized the screaming eagle on the forearm,
The mermaid's breasts on the bicep. Camels,
You said to yourself, and what had spiraled
That ticketman down to brake and lock, fast
Forward, and looking like he'd rape you
Or your sister or both on the Laff 'N Dark?
He might have been thinking, like you weren't,
That the Tumblebug was a sissy ride, that
It bumped and ground like women and would die
In five years like all of West View Park,
Its lake filled in with dirt so you could hike
To where your paddle boat had bumped against
A snag of stumps, so you could feel you were
Walking on water, that the soil was crust,
That the claws of your past could reach up
From the lost pudding of landfill beneath you.
And you could look at the trace of shoreline,
Say, "Tumblebug, Tilt-A-Whirl, RoundUp, Whip-it;"
Hear how the romanticism of rise and spin,
Fall and lurch, is an art like needle and ink.
And even though you are thinking height, speed,
Vertical drop and centrifugal force as you head
To shore, leaping once and digging in your heels
Until it seems that all you are is a child,

Leap a second time like you've always needed to,
Disbelieving, relieved, and seeing yourself,
As always, from the front of the waiting line.

Six Kinds of Music,
The Wallpaper of Breasts

I thought I'd drive the seventy miles
To see my son, slouch in a dorm room
With six kinds of music, the pleasure
Of his wallpaper of breasts. His wild hair
Was jammed down his shirt; we said nothing while
We breathed together as he looked for shoes
And I thumbed through his college catalogue
As if it were *People* at the dentist.

I recognized Tom Petty, Prince, The Who.
I heard, when another door swung open,
The Fine Young Cannibals, and I could have
Asked my son who else was singing along
That hall, but he said, finally, "That guy
On the cover was arrested for rape,"
And I closed his core curriculum, looked
Again at the student in the sweatshirt,
The name of my son's school across his chest
To sell parents, because he was seated
In the stacks, a sense of scholarship.

I felt like the fool of the worthless deed,
The lunkhead of the nosedived junk bond.
That student's slick smile had beamed at us
Through a senior year of choices; I'd tried
To read the titles of the books bunched on

The shelf behind him and made jokes about
The fabricated pose of study, how
Two hundred catalogues we owned had been
Cloned like the white pillars, ivy, and
The quarter-hour chorus of carillons.

I wasn't sure what it meant to have
A rapist on that cover, see my son
In his sweatshirt across the lawn from
Where a new library was being built.
For all I knew, the girl lived in that dorm,
Had a copy of this catalogue
Among her books. "He's history," I heard.
"He's expelled." And one of the stereos,
At least, was softened, turned off, or the door
Of its owner's room was so unlikely
Thick it shut the sound inside like a hand
Insistent over an astonished mouth.

The Panic Warnings

The Night Warnings
Fierce with fear, sometimes, we are, the terror
For which we can't account, positing *dreams*,
Learning, at last, to say *awake, aware*,
As predicate adjectives for despair.

It's my heart, I confess, that yammers *wolf*
Through the self defense of sleep. It lunges
Me upright to sweat and asthmatic breath,
The awful wheezing that will precede death.

My head, in these moments, is meant for soup,
Something of worth cooked from this foolish bone—
The fluttering, short-circuited sheep's
Brain in this skull that cannot guard my sleep.

The Nature Warnings
The folklore of toadstools. The dark ice
That drops us to drowning. The unfortunate
Head shape of snakes. The interpretation
Of tripled leaves. The hourglass on the spider.
The sky's soot. Its rain. The unspotted
Red slaughter of our daily apples.

In the back lots of learning, along
Its railroad tracks, head down and dreaming,
We know the schedule for taking the slam

In the face from the locomotive bloodstream:
Bacteria, virus, the seven warning signs—
We grow hoarse; we cough; we so slowly
Heal we may signify invasion.

The varicose heart, the snap and crackle
In the brain, and this summer I'm laying rock
Like flat gravestones through my yard,
One more path of the nameless if I think them
The lost cemetery of the developer's site,
The military's markers, or the marble stretch
Of one more mass-visited plaque. And I kneel
To run my fingers over their surfaces,
Feeling for the names, thinking each crease
Could be clue, another nature warning
If I were willing to touch so carefully
I might poison myself with discovery.

The Numbered Warnings
In the lights my body signaled,
In the first electrode moments,
The green line for my pulse peaking
As it should on the monitor,
I could follow the arcade game
Of myself, distracted at once
By the red scorecard for my heart—
Seventy, sixty-five, sixty . . .
I saw it searching for my life span,
Counting back to what I'd reached.

Fifty-five, fifty, forty-five . . .
And I thought in one more year
I would see myself vanish, have
All of those regretted years blip
Backwards in the technological flash
Before my eyes. Thirty-five, thirty . . .
And sure enough I fainted and found
Myself, seconds later, lifted from
The lab floor, Lazarus diminished
To the measured sham-death of panic.
And there, in the out-of-danger time
Of recovery, I told the doctor
My rehearsal stories, how sleep
Is a plastic bag, and she
Fluttered beside those print-outs,
A nerveless, one-night moth.

Reversing the Warnings

*If trains attain high speeds, the passengers will be unable
to breathe and will die of asphyxiation—*
Dr. Dionysius Lardner (19th Century)

Begin in space.
Black out the passage to Neptune.
Turn the Mars missions back.
Switch Armstrong to Glenn to Shepard
To a toppling *Vanguard* on the launchpad.
Earthbound, forget jets; disremember
Biplanes and the dream of flight.
Concentrate on land.

Lose salt flats, highways, the rutted one-lanes.
Now you can go on to trains,
Listen to Dr. Lardner,
Test your breath on board the bullet.
When you're seated,
Forget what you've read
About the diebacks of fish and trees,
Chemistry's deadlines for the planet.
Switch off sense, instincts;
Unlearn the autonomic of the rhythmic heart.
Forget each one of your footspeeds.
Try sitting, then lying down;
Try perfectly still.
Then see if you're moving too fast
To prevent the dieback of your race.
Then test your lungs with a mirror.
See if you're receding,
If arm's length is elastic,
That no wonder
There's no grading the breath test,
The calibration of fog.
In a moment you'll feel yourself
Riding that train,
Out-of-the-body observer, breathless.

The Drug Warnings

We've learned to be pleased if we swallow. We've learned to say,
"yes" and "all right" when the evening is a cellar, when all the
footsteps are above us. The track lighting near the stairs casts

four shadows of anything that forgets to blacken the house. An octopus reaches downstairs, or a spider, or the eight lives we've shed like foolish cats. Set and sewn by sheet lightning, the brain that Igor brought has been planted among us. In the Gothic Novel of our nights, we might as well stoop and scurry, mutter "master," and think ourselves whole. When the whimsy of the unbearable lurches forward, what can we do with raised fists and torches?

The Asbestos Warnings
In the building where I work, asbestos,
A week to remove it, assurances
That no one is in danger. These men know
Excision, joking scalp and stitch, dropping
The plastic shield from the ceiling, roping
Us out with the crime-scene ribbon. CAUTION,
It mutters, ASBESTOS, repeats itself
Wall-to-wall like a foul weather alert
Underlining a television show.

I'm paying attention; I'm staying home
This week and next, sure this curtain's useless,
Though, God knows, I've stopped to watch five minutes
(No longer), thinking these workers look like
All those women in showers who get slashed
When the curtain's yanked aside by psychos.
And all of the women who work here, who
Handle books for a living, are passing
In showers of their own, trusting, I guess,

The safety memo, the company's smile.
And each of these men goes home and showers.
They stand under water and aren't afraid
When somebody opens the bathroom door—
A wife, a lover, never the crazed lunge
Of knife that splits a lung. I might as well
Have found CAUTION in the card catalog
Behind me, looking under F, counting
The Dewey System to my favorite fears
As if they were shelved, bound by yellow tape
Saying DO NOT ENTER like the warnings
We tear apart on our way to pleasure,
Pain, the old wisdom of impermanence.

After the Warnings
The silence and light at the end of panic,
The face of the hospice in the mirror—
Pale solitude, death stubble that seems gray,
Then white, then reasonable at last.

The breath evens like the post-front weather;
The body manages alone, pivots, and the dog
Shakes itself to false morning, watches me
Wait the distance shorter from wish to rest.

And when I return to the room it never enters,
It stands white and small in the doorway. And when
I splash and swim to the pillow, this werewolf
Circles and settles and sprawls on its thumping side.

Love In The Liver

Maybe this explains tattoos, some sailor
Swallowing three hours of beer before
The needle uses him: the woman on his bicep
Loves him when he drinks that steady, weeklong way.

At first, the body is harmless. I know
I laughed at the stupid culture that created
This claim, love in the liver, because I knew,
Glued to every breast, where my love was,

And though there's nothing printed on my arms
I've tried to open women like presents,
Unraveled myself nightly with alcohol,
And ignored how anatomy quiets lies.

In the liver's vicinity there is an ache
Just short of pain. Absolutely, I vow,
These habits must stop, equating everything
Unattainable with blood-rich symptoms.

Iridology

I'm sitting, for my birthday, with friends;
I'm drinking the bad beer they give me,
In friendship, each year, buying the worst
They can find and passing me cards full
Of skeletons, hooded phantoms, crones
Who beckon with evil, candled cakes.
What a summer—drought, heat, and singing
Under this sickle moon a season
Since my mother has died, my father
Begun calling to explain estates.
And lately, I've been reading a book
On twentieth century crackpots,
Constructing a list of quackeries.
So I tell this table the story
Of Bernard Jensen, saying, "Listen
To this one, iridology, death
In our eyes around the iris clock."
And of course they smile at my joke card,
Let me add, "There's one illness per flaw;
There's self-diagnosis in the edge
Of color from morning to midnight,
Failures in the organs, muscles, bones.
So Jensen claimed, so we need mirrors,
Crazy for health, to peer for problems."

I'm waiting for their laughs; I'm touching
Both eyes with the guns of my fingers

To show I'm laughing, too, knowing which
Parts of myself I suspect, locking
Last night's door to inspect according
To Jensen. And I'm not telling them
I followed his charts, found one-fifteen,
Left iris, my blur of weak vision;
Checked three o'clock, right iris, asthma
In the hairline crack. And then night's start—
Kidneys, bladder, liver, groin—transcript
For the self-inflicted pain. And Christ,
I turned to ten o'clock, right iris,
To confirm the face I've lost; I lurched
To eleven o'clock, sex impulse,
For one bright story before midnight
Where the chart chants, "Animation, life."
But I say, "Next summer, something worse,
Beer more badly brewed, bitter or flat
Or spoiled into birthday legend."
I gather their empties, joke, "What's
Cured with a case of half-quarts?" thinking,
Silent, nine o'clock, left iris, that
Sure it's in mirrors, on walls, across
Landscapes where features predict blossom
Or decay through the iris of the earth:
Wrecking ball, acid rain, chemical
Blight or nuclear war's midnight hour
On the doomsday clock, so much an eye
We examine its iris to read

The future of ourselves, set its hands
Forward, back, forward, back, fine tuning
The shadows that gather in our lungs.

Idioglossia

Suppose ourselves twins
like the Kennedy sisters,
seizured at birth, kept
out of sight like the brainless.
Needing to talk, what
would we babble but "Dabans,
du-ah, aduh, das,"
haunting each other like dogs
leashed to midnight lawns.
Wouldn't we use the tied-twin
speech we imagine
comes from the otherworldly
voices of the dead
who were close? And wouldn't we
be discontented
with translation and long for
a twin in ourselves,
and having none, turn sullen
with the childlike chance
of language? Like these choices—
soft *c* or hard *c*
or the consonant-melded
c of each peopled
continent where they explain
the world by folklore,
by myth, by revelation
and the metaphors

that make magic of saying,
leaving us stranded
like the aliens who take
the form of humans
but give themselves away by
making constant sense.

What The Doctor Said

He told me he'd been afraid
the dog, rescued from fire,
was entering tachycardia,
the pulse he heard red-lining
to the valve-knock knot of death.

Save it somehow, he'd said
to himself, helpless on the lawn,
the house fire soaked, its owners
in his kitchen with coffee, a phone.

The night was returning to black;
his house was whole, its wiring
sound, and the dog quivered
as if it had turned to heart,
fibrillating in the grass.

He thought, finally, of the dart
and dash of small dogs, the sprint-pulse
of his sons. He and the dog
were as safe as newsmen
in the driveway. Though he sat
there anyway, like a father
in a waiting room, a magazine
closed on his lap as if he'd just
finished reading its feature spread.

The Fossil Route

Wagering the Sample
I was practicing Why me's?
Hearing terminal in a doctor's
Assurance words. Hadn't he just
Suggested death, that kidney stones
Weren't the shadows the brain
Refuses? I had myself under
The knife, conjured a soul
For myself who was slouched
Outside with black coffee
And a magazine, sure he could
Finish "Elvis Lives in Brazil"
Before he wagered another
Sample in a cup. I wasn't
Resilient as The King. My voice
Hadn't gone platinum or gold,
But my panic was the white
Of all colors for fear though
That doctor insisted I could
Walk away intact. Brilliant
With collapse, I knew he was
Drunk or drugged or delivering
Dreams. I couldn't shut myself up:
No matter what he denied, I talked
And talked, thinking I'll get to it,
What it is I'm working up to.

In the Fall of Fourth Grade

We found arrowheads in the woods, fossils
Among the stones of its creek, and we searched
For burial mounds, for the holy skulls
Of men, women, and children we'd unearth.
We talked, while we hunted, back the time line
To Pilgrims, Vikings, and the migration
Of people like apes. Which explanation
For our lives would we find? Which familiar
Tale would fit those bones like tissue and shine
Through the eyes like *certain, no doubt,* and *sure?*

This Thing

Before the CAT-scan, before the nurse had
My kidneys on film, she said, "You look good,"
Like women I'd dream. She meant my chances,
The odds my way because I didn't show
Symptoms in my face, but I let her pour
Iodine in me, and I held my breath
As if her fingers would verify me,
As if they were lasers to search and name.
I didn't want mistakes made. Whatever
I had or didn't have, I wanted things
Clear and that woman to trace them. And then
I was dressing myself again. Slowly.
The clothes I was putting on seemed stranger
That the clinic's gown. I sat and listened
To a man coughing in the next closet.

"Goddamn this thing," he said, and I agreed.
Once I knotted my shoelaces, I had
Doctors to see. About this thing. Or that.

The Geography of Climbing
And once, when houses were
coming to those woods,
we entered the huge pipe
laid into the earth
like a throat, and we turned
miners, rapped the walls

like the trapped, listened
for coded answers from
the solitary
confinement of shale.
We straddled water,
and like an A-student

I said, "Bay of Fundy,"
thought, "Dumb way to drown."
In the geography
of climbing, we were
Noah's odd pair—in case
of flood, no marriage

to save us. Always,
a disaster buries
The Lost World—earthquake,

tidal wave, volcano—
the monsters we seek
must die when we find them.

The Juried Art of Kidneys
Now I've heard a specialist say, "cancer,"
With my CAT-scan on his screen, learned, for sure,
You can listen to such language, answer
As if this were one more swabbed throat culture,
Another case of strep, the cross-sections
Of my kidneys hanging like juried art.
I've heard myself say, "I understand," start
Accepting, like the fool who waives his rights,
Medicine's justice, the skewed connection,
As if rage were synonym for polite.

The Fossil Route
I go out, in early
December, to dig
a hole for our bulbed tree,
anticipating,
for once, the frozen turf
of January.

I mean to improve
our landscape, choose the lawn's
largest bare spot, and
discover, three inches

below the surface,
a shelf of stone, something

to lift and throw until
it slants down like
an avenue leading,
for all I know, bent
on the shovel, cursing,
to the earth's center.

Sledge hammer and pick—
I could be forming
a grave in my yard,
and I fail, finally,
to budge that fossil route
to the world's lost core.

The Platitudes for Bees

I watch my daughter slap and run,
Slap and run, stuttering her fear
Across the yard like sentences
Beginning with explosive *p*'s,
And I open the door and call
The platitudes for bees, ending
With "Hurry, get inside," seeing
How invasion will make me stone.
She cries, is safe, stung only twice
And not allergic to this luck.
I tell her that someone survived
Two thousand bee stings; I tell her
This swarm believes she is doomsday,
And she backs away with knowing
The mind can be gutted by fear,
The body turned to flail and flap
And foolish words. We trip headlong
Into the scald-shock of each day,
And I feed her the strange stories
From my reading another book
Of limits, the best or the worst
Of something, like fences, like doors
To close quickly, thick sliding glass
That frames this needlepoint of bees.

The Cloth Flowers

They last like none of the others,
Like flags on the veterans' graves,
One kind of respect this morning
As I stand beside my father
Who brings gladiolas because
It's August, because the flowers
In his gardens vary from March
To November, because he weaves
A wreath in December that does
Evergreen work until crocus
Climbs out of the snow. He takes me,
Finally, past my mother's grave,
Twenty feet to the cloth flowers,
Says, "Touch them," and I do, thinking
These roses are dresses, almost
Erotic, that the nearest flag,
When it dreams, wishes itself placed
So close to these two-toned petals
They might open. My father waits,
Expects me to find a story
Here, the abstraction in the cloth,
And I, for once, approve, thinking
Asters, thinking September, and
What of the rain on these roses,
Their cloth voices garbled by stain
Or mold, and, if not, what treatments
They have taken to guarantee

One viewing season. So stable,
These Dorian Grays of flowers,
So permanent, these stay and stay.

The Double Negatives of the Living

After the pastor spoke well,
After he opened our route
With syntax and grammar
Correct as his manner,
I could follow my mother
To her grave and lapse into
The double negatives
Of the living. I could talk
Two hours past midnight with
My father in the steelworker
Idiom of his city, hearing
The fried mush of morning,
The white Sunday silence,
The many tongues of the cross
Speaking dialect stories
Of the holy mill. I could catch
His punctuation by breath born
In the thick ash of evening,
Overhear the end stops in
His coughs, the accidental case
For the thrift store's stock,
The body's swift tumors;
The chance of modifiers
For the factory uncles,
The fat, baking aunts,
The grandmothers in the pews
Of their dead husbands

Or rocking on porches
Flush with the brutal streets.
And finally the commas for
Steel, rivers, bridges, bars.
And Christ, the Expletive,
And all of the language
Of the land that we leave
And return to, reopening
The earth and stammering
Like the past's twin-speech,
What we know by repeating,
What runs on without us.

About the author

Gary Fincke is the author of two previous books of poetry, *Plant Voices* and *The Days of Uncertain Health*. In 1991 he was awarded the Bess Hokin Prize from *Poetry*. He is an Associate Professor of English and the Men's Tennis Coach at Susquehanna University in Selinsgrove, Pennsylvania where he lives with his wife, Liz, and their three children.